Positive behaviour support:
A brief guide for schools

Mark Wakefield and Sharon Paley

British Library Cataloguing in Publication Data
A CIP record for this book is available from the Public Library

© BILD Publications, 2011

BILD Publications is the imprint of:
British Institute of Learning Disabilities
Campion House
Green Street
Kidderminster
Worcs
DY10 1JL

Telephone: 01562 723010
Fax: 01562 723029
E-mail: enquiries@bild.org.uk
Website: www.bild.org.uk

No part of this book may be reproduced without prior permission from the publisher, except for the quotation of brief passages for review, teaching or reference purposes, when an acknowledgement of the source must be given.

ISBN 978 1 905218 13 4

Printed in the UK by Latimer Trend and Company Ltd, Plymouth

BILD Publications are distributed by:
BookSource
50 Cambuslang Road
Cambuslang
Glasgow G32 8NB
Telephone: 0845 370 0067
Fax: 0845 370 0068

For a publications catalogue with details of all BILD books and journals telephone 01562 723010, e-mail enquiries@bild.org.uk or visit the BILD website www.bild.org.uk

The British Institute of Learning Disabilities is committed to improving the quality of life for people with a learning disability by involving them and their families in all aspects of our work, working with government and public bodies to achieve full citizenship, undertaking beneficial research and development projects and helping service providers to develop and share good practice.

Contents

About the authors	4
Introduction	5
Behaviour that challenges	6
What makes behaviour worthwhile?	8
The principles of positive behaviour support	10
Taking positive action	12
Strategies for the classroom	15
In summary	21

About the authors

Mark Wakefield

Mark is a qualified teacher with over 14 years' experience of working with pupils who have been excluded from mainstream education. Previously a headteacher within a pupil referral unit, he now works as an independent consultant within schools and social care offering support and advice related to positive behaviour support, behaviour risk assessment and policy development.

Sharon Paley

Sharon is currently the development manager for positive behaviour support at BILD and also works as an independent consultant and trainer. She is a qualified nursery nurse and started her career working as a nursery nurse in special schools. Later training as a nurse for people with learning disabilities, she has worked in services for adults, children and young people.

Introduction

Teaching takes place in the context of relationships, most importantly those between staff and pupils, but also staff to staff and pupil to pupil. Behaviour is used within the context of these relationships to communicate all manner of things such as: happiness, pain, boredom, discomfort, trepidation, joy and fear.

Our ability to understand this communication is part of the relationships we build with the individual and is paramount to our success as teachers. We learn best when we are in a positive frame of mind – happy – a constant fear of consequence leads to anxiety and poor performance.

Positive behaviour support (PBS) is a tool that can enable us to better understand those we work with and build stronger relationships that allow us to more effectively communicate new ideas and information and so enhance the learning experience. It also leads to more positive learning environments in general, which as a consequence leads to a reduction in challenging behaviours.

This booklet offers a quick guide to the principles of PBS for teachers, classroom assistants and others working within a school environment. It is hoped that it provides an easy to read guide that will encourage you to find out more about PBS and how it can be implemented within a whole school setting. It is likely that the information may also be useful to people working in other settings with children and young people.

Behaviour that challenges

Behaviour may be described as challenging because it:

- is found to be difficult to manage or understand
- presents a risk to the pupil, other pupils, teachers or others
- is not appropriate for the environment in which it is being exhibited
- is inappropriate given the pupil's age or developmental ability

Primarily, children and young people who use behaviour to challenge a school setting are in some degree of distress. They are trying to communicate to us that their needs are not being met or they are experiencing some difficulties. In schools it is often the case that we are educating large groups of pupils without necessarily understanding them as individuals. There are many pupils who may have a mild learning disability, autism, attention deficit hyperactivity disorder (ADHD) or communication difficulties that are undiagnosed.

The reasons why children and young people may present us with a challenge include:

- family breakdown
- bereavement and loss
- illness
- use of recreational drugs or alcohol
- poor communication skills
- developmental difficulties

This is not a comprehensive list, but provides some reasons as to why children and young people may express themselves through their behaviour. It is always important to consider the child as an individual and to understand their perspective and identify their needs. It is important not to label pupils by either their behaviour or as a 'naughty' or 'disruptive' child. Labelling a pupil will establish an expectation of how they will behave and is against the basic philosophy of PBS.

What makes behaviour worthwhile?

We all behave in certain ways because it works for us! We gain something from those behaviours and so we continue to use them, sometimes for a long period of time, even when we recognise that they may be bad for us or our health. If a certain type of behaviour becomes part of our personal identity, and how we believe we relate to other people and them to us, it is much harder to stop. Behaviour is most worthwhile when it occurs in the context of our interaction with other people. For children and young people often the most important influences in their lives are their peers and adults with whom they have regular contact.

Behaviour may be worthwhile or work for a child or young person because they:

- gain sensations – perhaps the behaviour enables the pupil to feel elated or experience other sensations that they find enjoyable

- avoid sensations – it may be that the classroom environment is too noisy, too hot or too cold and the behaviour enables the pupil to escape the situation

- avoid tasks – the pupil may find certain lessons or tasks difficult and knows that exhibiting the behaviour will mean they can avoid the lesson

- experience emotional and cognitive conflict – this may be a totally irrational belief, for example a feeling of failure they feel when trying to access school work. Exhibiting a behaviour may be a way to express this feeling

- avoid people – social avoidance can be quite common in very young children or children who have developmental delay; tasks that require co-operation with others may be difficult and this can lead to avoidant behaviours

- obtain tangibles – the child or young person knows that the behaviour will gain a tangible 'reward'; it may be something they can use or particularly like, such as the opportunity to read a book or watch a DVD

- interact and communicate – the behaviour may be the primary way the child or young person has of interacting with others, usually because they do not have the skills or ability to build the relationships in more positive ways. A child may also be using their unacceptable behaviour to communicate an unmet need

In essence, children and young people initially act instinctively; if this has a desired outcome they will use the behaviour again. Quite quickly this behaviour becomes central to their communication and they will continue to use what has worked for them in the past and will keep doing it until it works again. As they get older these behaviours can increase in frequency and intensity, and are used quite skilfully by the young person.

In educational settings staff are presented with behaviours that may have had several years to become central to the young person's interactions with others and to their own identity. As a consequence, the person is often seen as and labelled by the behaviour rather than the behaviour being just one aspect of their personality. By using PBS we aim to identify those behaviours and understand the use or function of the behaviour(s) to the child or young person in order to facilitate more positive ways of communicating. Some behaviour used by pupils may seem bizarre or inappropriate given their age. However, bearing in mind that there may be other issues affecting them, we may need a deeper understanding of their difficulties to explain what is happening.

The principles of positive behaviour support

Positive behaviour support (PBS) is a value-driven approach; in implementing PBS it is important to focus on the individual and identify their needs. The most important aspect is to focus on the relationship we develop with the child or young person. A school that implements PBS throughout will value all pupils equally while accepting their individual differences and needs. This will promote self-esteem and pride within the whole school community. It is more than just a technique or strategy; it is a cultural ethos that supports many different objectives and achievements.

PBS:

- **is value driven**: implementing PBS strategies will include accepting that all pupils can contribute equally to the life of a school and the school community
- **is about positive communication**: PBS can increase the use of positive terminology and place an emphasis on appropriate communication – this should be supported across the school for all pupils and team members

- **appreciates the interaction between the individual and their environment**: understand how the child's life experiences, home life, school life and social experience affect them and how they express themselves through their behaviour
- **increases independence**: while acknowledging the developmental stage or age of a pupil it is important to focus on developing the child or young person's independence. Opportunities for pupils to 'practise' the things they are good at will heighten their personal sense of achievement and promote emotional and social wellbeing
- **promotes emotional literacy**: ensure that children and young people have opportunities to express themselves and help and support them to understand their own feelings
- **creates a positive environment**: schools should be welcoming for all pupils. It is important to acknowledge each pupil's individuality, culture and life experience so that they feel they are valued and important members of the school community
- **focuses on individual support**: each pupil is an individual and pupils will respond more positively if they are addressed by name and the curriculum meets their developmental and educational needs. Behaviour support should also be targeted to address the specific needs of individual pupils as opposed to a group of pupils
- **works towards achievable goals**: set goals that will motivate and are achievable within a timescale that is reasonable given the age and developmental level of the children or young person

Taking positive action

It is possible to introduce some simple strategies that will help support the implementation of PBS in your school, including:

- **getting to know each pupil as an individual**: talk to them about the things that interest them, no matter how trivial or unimportant they may seem to you. Communicating with children and young people about the things that matter to them will help form positive relationships. This will also enable you to form a better understanding of the pupil. Listening to the language they use; noting their use of body language and their topics of conversation may give indicators to their ability levels and underlying issues, such as family problems that may not have been communicated to the school

- **ensuring the whole staff team understand the principles of PBS and appreciate the beneficial outcomes that it will achieve**: ensure that all the staff are engaged in the process and being consistent. Like any process if a minority of staff fail to use the principles then it starts to make life difficult for the majority. Consistency is the key

- **forming positive relationships with pupils and use positive language**: be approachable and engaging. We all have better relationships with people that take an interest in us and show some desire to know about us. In this context, by responding positively to pupils we, in turn, are more likely to be responded to in a positive way

- **setting clear expectations and rules**: make sure all pupils are aware of the school's rules and present them in a way that all the pupils can understand. Some children will naturally push at boundaries that have been imposed. However, the clearer the expectations are the less room for manoeuvring on the part of the pupil

- **having clear consequences that apply to all the pupils**: don't single out or apply differing consequences to pupils who challenge the rules. Children have an innate sense of fairness and will expect those rules to be followed by everyone. It is often the failure to keep to guidelines and boundaries by staff that can prove frustrating to the pupil and lead to extremes of behaviour

- **be honest and sincere in your communications and actions**: if you make a promise follow it through. Don't say one thing and communicate something entirely different in your actions or through your body language. If this happens it amounts to a breakdown in the relationship between the pupil and staff member. The loss of trust that occurs in this situation may take many weeks or months to rebuild

- **showing that you are concerned about them and care about the welfare of the children**: in the context of a positive relationship this will lead to a better understanding of the individual and increase the likelihood of that child or young person feeling confident enough to turn to a member of staff should they require help in the future

- **being aware of achievement and praising the child, no matter how small the achievement may be**: as adults it is easy to overlook some achievements, merely seeing them as age appropriate or that a child is just doing what they were expected to do. For some children the praise you provide may be the only praise they get day to day. Do not underestimate the importance of this in building a pupil's self-esteem and the impact this may have in positively supporting your relationship with them

- **acknowledging appropriate behaviour and thinking about catching the child or young person doing positive things**: we need to think in broader terms here than just the context of their school work. For example, Jimmy may have just said 'thank you' to Billy who he doesn't normally get along with. Catching this and using it positively is at the heart of the PBS process. With any praise and reward system we need to be sensitive to the pupil's understanding. How many pupils have ripped-up work when told it is a good piece? If the pupil doesn't understand how to accept this praise we need to find appropriate ways to engage, reward and develop their understanding. Just displaying the piece of work without mentioning it to the child will show them that you value them and their work without them having to accept the praise directly

- **being clear about school routines, especially when they are likely to change for any reason**: when routines are to change give a warning and explain why the routine will change and how it will change. We can all find changes in routine difficult to deal with. The better informed we are the more able we are to prepare for what is going to happen. We need to bear in mind that for some pupils the process of change is an extremely difficult one to manage and we need to provide them with the skills and structure in which to develop this

- **creating a positive environment that is welcoming to children and their family**: if the whole family feels welcome within the school this will enable the pupil to be supported by everyone who is important in their life. It will also create opportunities to share information with the pupil's family. The importance of good relationships with families cannot be underestimated. Getting parents 'on side' can be an invaluable tool to help a child develop more appropriate coping strategies. When parents or carers find it difficult to have contact with the school on a regular basis, the importance of consistency within the school setting increases as the pupils' experiences out of school may differ considerably

Strategies for the classroom

1. Use behaviourally specific language

An important element of PBS is the use of behaviourally specific language; simply telling a child or young person their behaviour is naughty is unhelpful and judgemental. Describing the behaviour as 'unacceptable' and accompanying this with a reason is much more helpful to pupils, and will reinforce the expectations you have of them.

For example, two children are play fighting in the playground. They believe this is a game. If you simply tell them 'not to play like that' they may think they have been told off for playing. It is important to explain why they must not play fight and how one of them may be injured as a consequence. Then, give them an alternative such as 'Why not have a race, the first one back to me gets a merit!' And then reward both children with a merit.

2. Acknowledge positive behaviour often and as much as possible

It is very helpful to acknowledge and reward positive behaviour. Do not point out those not following the rules; reward those pupils who are. Recognising the pupils who 'do what is expected of them' is important.

For example, when a pupil follows a classroom rule it will be important to acknowledge that they have understood the rule and followed the rule well. It is particularly important to praise pupils when they do things for each other or are considerate of others. Praising socially acceptable behaviour will build important social skills and contributes towards a positive school community. Ensure that the praise used is appropriate to the individual. Occasionally pupils will not like a comment made to the whole class on their positive behaviour. Alternative strategies can be useful, maybe a light tap on the shoulder or nod may be enough to acknowledge the pupil's achievement.

3. Good communication

Good communication and clear instructions are particularly important. You may be one of just two adults in the classroom; remember a child is one of many. It can be very difficult to understand instructions when they are muddled or given to a collective group. In particular, some children with developmental disabilities, such as autism or ADHD, may not understand that group instructions are meant for them. Some children need help to practise their 'listening' skills or reciprocal communication skills.

It's easy to forget that children see themselves as one of many in a busy classroom. For some children the environment can be overwhelming. For example, a pupil may often miss important instructions because they are not used to following instructions. In a group situation this may get worse as they are easily distracted by other children or may 'act out' in order to gain peer approval. In these instances it may be useful to have a written set of instructions that the pupils can follow. Try to do more than just write these up on the board as some pupils may have sight difficulties they are not aware of or unwilling to disclose. Well differentiated lesson planning will help with this task. It is particularly important here to ensure you are aware of the pupils' individual education plans (IEPs), which may be in place to take account of the difficulties that are **known**.

4. Set achievable goals

Set reasonable and achievable goals for the pupil and make reasonable adjustments for individual pupils dependant on their age, developmental level, stage of learning and learning style. Pupils will feel happier and gain a sense of self-worth if they achieve targets on a regular basis and are able to make progress.

Adjust activities for pupils so that they can easily reach a target and enjoy learning; often children who use unacceptable behaviour have difficulty in managing school work. If the targets are broken down into manageable tasks the pupil will see the task as more attainable and then enjoy new opportunities for learning and their problematic behaviour may become less worthwhile.

Another useful point to remember is that we often reward good work with more work! Pupils who complete work on task are often given more to do. When tasks are set ensure that the pupils understand what is expected of them. Don't then ask them to do more. For some pupils this could be the trigger for a behaviour outburst. You can gradually increase the amount of work expected of an individual once you know their strengths and have identified how to best support their learning style and developmental level.

5. Create a positive environment

Ensure that the classroom is welcoming for pupils and appropriate to their age. Give pupils space, time and adequate equipment. Also ensure that there is sufficient space for pupils to move about without them 'bumping' into each other – crowded environments can lead to behaviour that may be disruptive to learning. It's also important to make equipment available to pupils or this may offer an excuse for them to move about a classroom causing disruption.

If the classroom is welcoming, children and young people will want to be there, no one likes to be in an environment that is shabby or unwelcoming! It places a value on the activities that take place in the school if it is bright, airy and well decorated. Make sure all pupils have access to equipment they need, there may be an expectation that older pupils supply some equipment. Don't make undue fuss if they don't have the equipment, this will set up conflict (it may be beyond their control or is their way of taking control). Provide equipment and remind them of their responsibility. Importance must be placed on the pupil taking part in lessons alongside their peers. Of course, issues of space may be beyond your control, but otherwise the environment is yours to decide. It may mean a rearrangement of seating and tables is required but this is often a good way to make a positive impact on the pupils' behaviours.

6. Set clear rules, consequences and responsibilities

Set clear classroom rules, consequences and responsibilities. These must be adapted so that they are appropriate for the age and developmental stage that the children are at and be appropriate to the environment.

Involve the children in setting the classroom rules; this will help them to develop a sense of ownership and co-operation. Ask them their opinions on the rules and the consequences for pupils who do not follow the rules. Children are often very harsh in their setting of consequences for breaking rules. Their involvement in the planning of rules will help them to accept their use when they need to be applied and understand their fair use. Involving children in the daily life of the school, by sharing responsibility with them, can be very useful in encouraging acceptable behaviours. Responsibilities may include: giving books out, taking a register to another classroom, supporting younger pupils or helping other pupils with a task.

7. Be consistent

Be consistent in your approach to pupils. Children and young people like to 'know where they stand'. If you are inconsistent, pupils will not know where they are and they will feel that people are being treated differently.

Be consistent in how you communicate with pupils, be clear about the expectations you have of them and follow through on promises you make, especially if they are viewed as positive 'rewards' by the pupils. Also, be consistent between pupils. Although you may have to differentiate in terms of meeting the needs of individual pupils, their learning styles and rewards that will act as motivators, it's important to be aware that you are not seen to be favouring any one pupil over another. For example, rewarding pupils for completing work is based upon the work they have been set individually and is not based upon a common set amount. This can be seen as fair and consistent as, individually, they have completed their tasks. It is also important not to negate some pupils' positive achievements on the basis that one member of the group did not complete a task. This would be perceived as unfair by the pupils and may lead to challenging behaviour from some, and a breakdown in the pupil/staff relationship leading to other issues in the classroom.

Working with the individual pupil

Some pupils (very few) will have a range of behaviours that may be difficult to manage in a school setting. Some pupils may also be experiencing a range of difficulties and emotions, which is why they are using behaviour as a means to communicate how they are feeling and express themselves. If this is the case, it is important to:

- reassure the pupil that they are important and valued as a person
- remind them of the school/class rules
- change the classroom environment, perhaps where the pupil is sitting, remove items that trigger the behaviour
- involve the child's parents or carers in any planning
- introduce a pupil contract if the child/young person can understand the concept
- give options and choices; don't 'back the child/young person into a corner'
- use re-direction when you recognise the pupil's behaviour is escalating; direct them to another activity or offer another option
- reward acceptable behaviour and achievements as often as possible

For these pupils it is important to develop individual behaviour support plans. The aim of such a support plan is to:

- accurately describe the behaviour(s) and undertake a holistic assessment of the behaviours that cause concern
- ensure that the behaviours are assessed and the function understood
- reduce the risk presented by the behaviour
- implement consistent approaches so that the staff team know how to best support the pupil
- describe strategies that will prevent the behaviour
- describe strategies for managing the behaviour

- reduce the impact that the behaviour has on the pupil and those who are friends with them or teach them
- reduce reliance on aversive management strategies such as restrictive physical interventions, which have **no place** in a PBS plan
- reduce the impact that the behaviour(s) has/have on the pupil(s); their opportunities for learning and developing socially and emotionally

In Summary

Implementing positive behaviour support

This can only be a short guide to implementing some of the principles of PBS but, hopefully, it will encourage and support you to develop some new approaches and perhaps explore the key concepts in more detail.

If you implement PBS, it will:

- increase opportunities for the development of independence appropriate to the developmental level and age of the pupil
- enable the pupil to feel valued as a unique individual who has important relationships and is part of the school community
- enable the pupil to develop their communication and social skills, and increase opportunities for positive experiences
- support social and emotional development
- support all pupils to be part of the school community and to engage on an equal basis – value each pupil's contribution no matter how small
- increase opportunities for pupils to take personal responsibility for themselves and others
- increase opportunities for new learning experiences in a secure and safe environment
- support the pupil to develop an understanding of consequences and the impact of their actions on others
- create opportunities for fun and enjoyment, a sense of having something to look forward to

Do's

- Recognise individuals, you are the teacher of individual pupils not a subject, group, class or form
- Enable pupils to take ownership of their personal learning objectives and achievements
- Make learning fun and engage pupils in their learning
- Communicate effectively and set reasonable achievable goals for each pupil
- Prepare learning activities; make sure all the equipment is available to pupils – learning should be structured and have identifiable goals
- Acknowledge personal achievements of pupils
- Be positive at all times and avoid the use of judgemental language
- Recognise when you are wrong and acknowledge that adults can (and do) make mistakes
- Remember you are a role model, your behaviour will affect the behaviour of those around you and the relationships you form with them

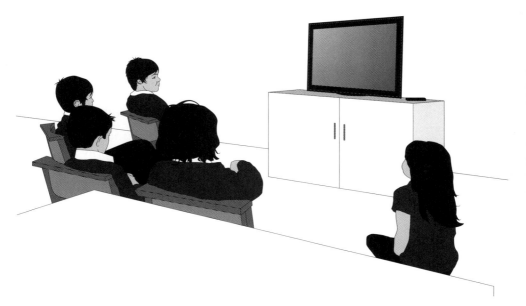

Don'ts

- Don't expect pupils to read your mind; give clear concise instructions and repeat them if necessary
- Don't raise your voice or lose control – this will undermine your relationship with pupils and they may not feel safe in your company if you behave in this way
- Don't use sarcasm or demean pupils or other staff members – this will undermine the development of positive relationships within the whole school community
- Don't hold a group of pupils collectively responsible for the unacceptable behaviour of one or two pupils; pupils will feel that this is unjustified and this will undermine their trust in you
- Don't single pupils out or personalise your communication by using nicknames or surnames of pupils – as a rule this will have a negative impact on the pupil and how they perceive their relationship with you as a responsible adult
- Don't keep confrontation going for the sake of it! Always give pupils a 'way out' without them losing face in front of their peers; remember you are the adult in the relationship

Positive behaviour support will be effective as a whole school approach. For maximum impact everyone must understand and adopt the principles and be consistent in the approaches used throughout the school community. Many of the principles discussed here will already be taking place within individual classrooms and across the school as a whole. Recognising they are and promoting them throughout the whole school is the aim.

To reduce reliance on behaviour management, a school will require good and clear leadership that places an emphasis on open and clear communication; empowerment of the staff team; development of the staff team and their skills; as well as emphasising a reduction in aversive practices.

The benefits will be an increase in the confidence of the staff team, consistent approaches across the school, clear expectations for pupils and improvements in the transition between academic years.